D1495883

Latinos in the Limelight

Christina Aguilera

Antonio Banderas

Jeff Bezos

Oscar De La Hoya

Cameron Diaz

Jennifer Lopez

Ricky Martin

Selena

CHELSEA HOUSE PUBLISHERS

LATINOS
IN THE
LIMELIGHT

Christina Aguilera

Susan Korman

CHELSEA HOUSE PUBLISHERS
Philadelphia

Frontis: *Singing sensation Christina Aguilera wows audiences around the world.*

Produced by
21st Century Publishing and Communications, Inc.
New York, New York
http://www.21cpc.com

CHELSEA HOUSE PUBLISHERS

Editor in Chief: Sally Cheney
Production Manager: Pamela Loos
Art Director: Sara Davis
Director of Photography: Judy L. Hasday
Managing Editor: James D. Gallagher
Senior Production Editor: J. Christopher Higgins
Publishing Coordinator: James McAvoy
Project Editor: Anne Hill

The Chelsea House World Wide Web address is
http://www.chelseahouse.com

First Printing

1 3 5 7 9 8 6 4 2

Library of Congress Cataloging-in-Publication Data

Korman, Susan.
   Christina Aguilera / Susan Korman.
      p. cm. – (Latinos in the limelight)
   Includes bibliographical references (p.).
   ISBN 0-7910-6106-X (hardcover) — ISBN 0-7910-6107-8 (pbk.)
      1. Aguilera, Christina, 1980– —Juvenile literature. 2. Singers—United States—
Biography—Juvenile literature. 3. Hispanic American singers—United States—
Biography—Juvenile literature. [1. Aguilera, Christina, 1980– . 2. Singers. 3. Hispanic
Americans—Biography. 4. Women—Biography.] I. Title. II. Series.

ML3930.A36 K67 2000
782.42164'092—dc21
[B]   00—059621
                                                                         CIP
                                                                          AC

CONTENTS

THE NOTE THAT
CHANGED HER LIFE

It was early 1998, and RCA Record Company executive Ron Fair was feeling optimistic. He'd just signed a development deal with a promising young singer.

In the music business, a development deal is one in which a record company agrees to work with a musician, to help develop her talent. Then, if the company is pleased by the artist's progress, they will go on to sign her to an actual record contract.

The singer whom Fair had just signed was a girl from Wexford, Pennsylvania, a suburb outside of Pittsburgh. She was young—only 17 years old. But Fair, the Artists and Repertoire director at RCA, was a seasoned music industry executive who had sharpened his instincts over the years. And this time his instincts were telling him that the girl from Pennsylvania was the real thing.

Fair had worked with some talented singers, including Natalie Cole, during his career, but he couldn't remember ever hearing such a powerful voice and astonishing range in someone so young. Fair was convinced that with the right training and the right material, this girl might someday be as popular as the Spice Girls or the Backstreet Boys.

The young singer was still on Fair's mind when his

Christina's stunning rise to fame was largely due to her amazing musical ability.

phone rang. On the line was an executive from Disney Studios. The movie company was about to release a new animated feature titled *Mulan*. Disney was looking for a female vocalist who could sing a ballad for the film's soundtrack. The singer had to be young, the Disney executive told Fair, but she also had to be able to hit a particularly high note—the third E-flat above middle C. Did Fair happen to know of a young singer with a wide vocal range?

Christina Aguilera, the name of the young singer from Pennsylvania, popped back into Fair's head. After hanging up with the caller from Disney, he quickly dialed Steve Kurtz, who was Christina's agent. Kurtz was another experienced businessman. He knew right away that this could be the big break his young client had been waiting for.

Kurtz soon learned that the staff at Disney was working on a very tight schedule. Unfortunately, this meant there would be no time to get Christina into a recording studio to tape a demo for Disney. However, Kurtz wasn't about to let this chance slip away. He quickly came up with a solution: Christina could record her demo at home.

Christina was thrilled when she heard about the job for Disney Studios. But before she let herself get too excited, she had work to do. She grabbed her boom box and plopped down in her family's living room to get started.

Christina had decided to tape a demo of herself singing "I Wanna Run to You." The song had first been recorded by Whitney Houston, a powerful female vocalist. Christina knew it was a good choice. "I Wanna Run to You" would showcase her strong voice and demonstrate her ability to reach the high note that Disney was looking for.

Christina took a deep breath and began. She

sang with deep emotion and the easy confidence of an accomplished star. After only one take, Christina was sure she'd nailed it. Trying to keep her excitement under control, she packaged up her homemade demo, then sent the tape off to Disney.

That night Christina didn't sleep much. Instead she tossed and turned, wondering what the Disney movie makers would think of her demo. What if her voice wasn't right for the song from the movie? What if the movie makers had found another vocalist, someone who was able to send a professional demo recorded in a real studio?

Luckily, Christina didn't have to wait long to find out what impression her demo had made. The Disney producers were so awed by her voice and range that they wanted her in Los Angeles right away! Just 48 hours after she'd packaged up the tape, Christina found herself in a recording studio in LA, taping the song "Reflection" for the soundtrack of *Mulan.*

No wonder Christina would later call that high E-flat "the note that changed my life." Her ability to reach the note landed her the job with Disney, which in turn sparked her meteoric rise to superstardom.

The animated movie *Mulan* is the story of a girl named Mulan who is coming of age in ancient China. When she learns that her elderly father has been ordered to help fight the Huns, she disguises herself as a boy and steps in to take his place. Eventually, Mulan manages to help defeat the enemy. Her brave and decisive actions bring glory to both her country and her family.

The song "Reflection" is in many ways the musical and emotional centerpiece of the film. In the song, Mulan sings about her search for her true identity, wondering who she is and how she fits into China's male-dominated society. The

Christina's compelling performance for the soundtrack of Mulan *led to her being offered a recording contract with RCA.*

song was written by Matthew Wilder and David Zippel. The heartfelt ballad was exactly the kind of song that Christina has always loved to sing.

Christina spent a week in the Disney studio in Los Angeles, perfecting the ballad for the movie's soundtrack. Each time she sang the song, its lyrics and soaring melody seemed to become a part of her. She poured her heart into the music and quickly managed to make the song her own. "The song's theme—the struggle to establish your identity—was something I could really relate to as a teenage girl myself," she said.

Christina was scheduled to fly home after her recording session. But instead she decided to stick around to hear the 90-piece orchestra that would accompany her voice on the final recording. "It was enough to bring tears to my eyes," she said later of the experience. "It was so amazing to hear that beautiful music."

When Christina finally left Los Angeles, she was thrilled. Any new movie from Disney was a major event, and she knew that she was about to be part of all the publicity and promotion surrounding the movie's premiere. She also knew that she was very lucky to have been given the opportunity. "Those kinds of things come along once every few years," she thoughtfully remarked later. "[Disney] took a huge chance using an unknown like me."

The movie *Mulan* premiered in June 1998, and "Reflection" became an instant hit. Suddenly, Christina's voice was playing on millions of radios across the country. She was also in constant demand, making live TV appearances to sing the song and promote the new movie for Disney.

But that wasn't the only source of her sudden success. RCA executive Ron Fair was also very aware of the significance of *Mulan*'s upcoming premiere. After hearing Christina's sensational recording of "Reflection," he decided that he'd been too cautious in signing her to just a development deal. That same week, he offered Christina her own recording contract with RCA. The young singer was no longer considered "in development." Now she was a full-fledged artist with a contract to make a whole CD of her own songs. Christina was in shock when she heard the fabulous news. Her dream had just come true—she was going to record her own album.

Christina was only a teenager when she became a star. In some ways her dizzying success felt surreal, like a dream. But in other ways, her sudden fame wasn't the least bit surprising. For as Christina and her family can testify, the little girl from Wexford, Pennsylvania, had been preparing for this moment almost from the day she was born.

2

THE LITTLE GIRL
WITH THE BIG VOICE

To a young couple like Fausto and Shelly Aguilera, Staten Island, New York, seemed the perfect place to buy a home. Housing prices were reasonable, and it was close to where Fausto was stationed in the U.S. Army. Even though the island itself was like a small town, the big-city lights of Manhattan were only a ferry ride away.

The year 1980 was an exciting time for Fausto and Shelly. They were not only buying a home but also expecting their first child. The baby was due in December, shortly before Christmas. Shelly was especially looking forward to settling down, at least for a little while. She knew Fausto's job in the army would always mean a lot of moves for their family. But for now they could stay put.

Fausto Aguilera was born in Ecuador. He and Shelly, who is Irish-American, met while she was studying to be a Spanish interpreter. But speaking Spanish wasn't Shelly's only talent. She was also an accomplished musician who could play both violin and piano. As a young girl Shelly had been a member of a youth symphony orchestra. She'd even toured Europe with the group.

On December 18, just one week before Christmas,

The big-city lights of New York are only a ferryboat ride away from Staten Island, where Christina was born.

Shelly gave birth to a baby girl, whom she and Fausto named Christina Maria. Everyone who saw the baby commented on her huge, luminous blue eyes.

As soon as she could talk, little Christina began to make music. According to Shelly, her little girl sang whenever she could. In the bath, she'd use a shampoo bottle as a pretend microphone. In her bedroom Christina would sing into a brush or a baton.

"She'd line up all of her stuffed animals," Shelly later told interviewers, "and sing to them with my little majorette baton that was her 'ikaphone.' She was too young to pronounce microphone! I've never seen anybody so focused."

It wasn't long before Christina's father was assigned to a new post. This time the family relocated to Florida, a move that was soon followed by transfers to Texas, Japan, and New Jersey.

By this time Christina had a younger sister, Rachel. There had been many changes so far in her young life, but one thing had stayed constant—Christina's love for singing. When friends came to call for her, her mother would often report that she was singing in her room. And when the family went out in public, Christina would also amuse herself by singing. Strangers who overheard her would look on in disbelief at the amazing sound of her voice. They couldn't believe that a little girl could sing with such maturity and style.

Christina especially loved singing soundtracks from Broadway musicals. By the time she was six, she'd memorized every song from *The Sound of Music*, the popular musical by

Richard Rodgers and Oscar Hammerstein III.

Christina sang for the sheer pleasure of it, but as she grew, music took on another purpose in her life. With each of the family's moves, the tension between her parents mounted. The family's constant relocation was a strain on Shelly, who longed to settle down and provide her daughters with a permanent home. Before long Fausto and Shelly concluded that the marriage wasn't working, and they divorced.

Christina was just seven years old at the time. Her parents' divorce had a traumatic effect on her. Singing was a natural way for her to relieve some of the stress and anxiety she felt.

After the divorce from Fausto, Shelly suddenly faced the task of raising two young daughters on her own. So she decided that the best thing to do was to move back to her hometown of Wexford, Pennsylvania, a suburb of Pittsburgh. It meant yet another move for the family. But she hoped that this one would help her daughters settle down and begin to establish roots.

Shelly, Christina, and Rachel moved in with Shelly's mother. Christina enjoyed living with her grandmother. She quickly became close to the older woman, who encouraged her to follow her dreams. Later Christina would remark to *Twist* magazine, "It was my grandma who said maybe this was something more than just a kid singing in the tub."

Christina's grandmother noticed that her granddaughter already knew popular music and songs from Broadway musicals. She decided to broaden Christina's musical education by introducing her to the blues, a jazz style of African-American origin. Together, they explored used record stories, trying to track down recordings by two famous blues vocalists—Billie Holiday and Etta James. Christina admired the two women's strong, resonant voices. One of her favorite songs, "At Last," was a ballad recorded by Etta James.

To those around her, it seemed as if Christina's talent was blossoming more each day. At eight years old, she was regularly belting out songs by the diva Whitney Houston at neighborhood parties and school talent shows. Everyone who heard her was amazed by her powerful voice. It was becoming increasingly apparent that the young schoolgirl had an extraordinary gift.

These early opportunities to sing in front of a group taught Christina something important: she loved to perform. It was fun to sing in her room or for her family, but it was a completely different experience to sing for a larger audience. She loved watching people respond so enthusiastically to the music she made.

Christina's appearances at parties and community events became more frequent. "If there wasn't a block party or somewhere for her to sing, she'd get irritable," Shelly joked later. People who heard her sing often came up to ask for her autograph. Many of them predicted that Christina would become a big star someday.

Christina hoped that these predictions would come true. In the meantime, she was definitely becoming a celebrity in her own town. Several articles about her appeared in local newspapers, and even the mayor of Pittsburgh asked her to perform. The director of the Pittsburgh Theater Company/Pohl

The recordings of legendary blues singer Billie Holiday, left, inspired Christina, who admired the vocalist's musical style and phrasing.

Productions remembers her as a "little girl with an adult voice. She was always the undefeated champion in talent shows."

Christina's talent continued to delight and astonish her mother. However, it also posed some problems. Shelly didn't want to stifle her daughter's natural gift, but she worried that Christina was being pushed too hard too soon. Shelly encouraged her to perform, but she also wanted her daughter to grow up like a normal kid.

Still, Christina remained very driven. Despite

her young age, she knew with certainty that she had been born to sing. "I wanted to perform for as long as I could remember," she later told reporters.

Around this time Christina heard about an exciting announcement in the local newspaper. Auditions for a television talent show, *Star Search*, were going to be held in Pittsburgh. *Star Search* was a popular TV show in the 1980s. Hosted by a celebrity named Ed McMahon, the program featured people from around the country who had special talents. They competed for cash prizes and hoped that this would be their chance to be discovered. Several well-known personalities, such as comedienne and talk-show host Rosie O'Donnell, went on to become famous after appearing on *Star Search*. Christina begged her mother to let her audition for an appearance on the show, and Shelly agreed.

Christina was nervous when she and her mother walked into the Pittsburgh audition. The waiting room was filled with other children who were hoping to win a spot on the show. Many of them were kids her age. But Christina was hoping that her big voice, which was so mature for an eight-year-old, would set her apart from the other young contestants.

When Christina's name was finally called, her heart pounded. She hurried onto the stage, where the bright spotlights shone on her. As she began to sing, her nervousness disappeared. She was so intensely involved in singing, all she was aware of was the song.

At last the tryout was over. The *Star Search* producers told the contestants that they would be notified of the results within a few days. The contestants also learned that if

Christina is used to staying poised while performing in front of thousands of fans. At only eight years old, she already knew how to set her fears aside while under the spotlight.

they made it past this round, the next step would be to compete against another round of regional contestants. After that, anyone who made it would be flown out to Los Angeles to compete on the actual show.

The next few days were agonizing ones for Christina. She tried to forget about the *Star Search* audition and concentrate on school and her friends. But it was close to impossible for the excited little girl to put the show out of her mind. It seemed as if her entire future rested on the *Star Search* producers.

STAR SEARCH

A t last the envelope from the producers of *Star Search* arrived in the mail. With trembling fingers, Christina opened it. She'd made it! She was one of the few contestants who had reached the next round.

Christina knew this was good news. But she was also aware that she'd have to compete again—against all of the other first-round winners—in order to win a spot on the show. This time the competition would be very intense. Many of the other singers would be quite talented.

When it came time for the next round, once again Christina was nervous. But she remained poised and as she stood on stage to perform for the judges, she focused on the music, and her confidence quickly returned.

Christina was glad that the contestants didn't have a long wait this time around. The judges announced the results after everyone had performed. Once again Christina had made it. She was going to compete on the *Star Search* television show.

Christina returned home to Wexford, very excited. She'd

Ed McMahon, the show's host, introduces the audience to Star Search, *a talent competition for young hopefuls. Christina was beside herself with excitement when, after her first performance, she received the news that she had advanced to the next round of the competition.*

competed against some very talented singers and won. Plus, the show was paying to send her to Los Angeles, where the program was taped. She'd be picked up by a limousine and put up at a fancy hotel, just like a real star.

Christina and her mother had a wonderful time in California. The night before the show was taped, they ate at restaurants and toured Hollywood. Seeing the sights of this glamorous city where so many famous people lived was a thrill for Christina.

The next day was a busy one. Christina had to attend a *Star Search* rehearsal in the morning. Then in the afternoon, the show was taped before a live audience. As Christina listened to the other singers and gazed about at the TV cameras, her nervousness grew. She had to admit that there were a lot of other really talented kids. The judges would be watching and listening very closely to her performance—and so would millions of other people when the show appeared on TV.

Christina took the stage and began to sing. She was performing one of her favorites, "The Greatest Love of All," a Whitney Houston song. Her performance, as always, was strong and impressive. Afterward, Christina huddled backstage with the other contestants, anxiously awaiting the judges' decision.

When it came, Christina burst into tears. She'd come in second place. The first-place prize was given to a 12-year-old boy who sang "Hey There, Lonely Girl," a song by Eddie Holman.

Christina was devastated. Even though she'd known the competition would be fierce, she'd still hoped so much to win the first prize. Shelly hugged her daughter, then prodded her to go over and congratulate the winner. With tears still streaming down her face, Christina went over and shook the boy's hand.

When Christina returned home, her friends and family were very proud. Even though she herself was disappointed about coming in second, others from her hometown were impressed that the girl from Wexford had made it so far.

Christina went back to school, eager to talk about her *Star Search* experience. But unfortunately, this was the beginning of a very painful lesson for the singer. She began to see that fame and success often carry a steep pricetag.

Instead of being pleased for her, many of Christina's classmates were jealous. Several kids and their parents shunned her. Others made fun of her, teasing her about her powerful voice and theatrical singing style. Christina couldn't understand why so many people seemed to be so resentful of her. It was a difficult and lonely time.

Christina hoped that things at school would improve over time. Instead, the situation only grew worse. One day, the family discovered that the tires on her mother's car had been slashed. Mother and daughter made a difficult decision: Christina would transfer to another school.

While this was a stormy period in the young singer's life, it also strengthened her resolve and determination to succeed. "I always envied people who had childhood friends and memories of growing up together because I never really had that," she wistfully recalled later on. "The divorce and the hard times at school, all those things combined to mold me, to make me grow up quicker. And it gave me the drive to pursue my dreams that I wouldn't necessarily have had otherwise."

Christina gradually settled into her new

school, making new friends. With the money she'd won from *Star Search,* she purchased a small public address system that she could use for local performances. She also continued listening to music whenever she got a chance.

In 1990, a new artist named Mariah Carey released her first album. Christina was in awe of the vocalist's technique and style, which she called a "breath of fresh air." At the time, grunge music and "gangsta" rap were very popular. Christina was glad to suddenly hear someone with such a beautiful voice on the radio. She liked to sing the same type of soaring ballads that Mariah sang so well.

By this time Pittsburgh's three professional sports teams—Steelers, Penguins, and Pirates— had heard about the young girl from Wexford with the big voice. They asked Christina to sing the national anthem before some of their games. She was more than happy to oblige.

One day Christina's mother spotted another ad in the newspaper. The Disney Company was looking for performers for a new show, *Mickey Mouse Club.* The program was modeled after *The Mickey Mouse Club,* a variety show from the 1950s. Disney was going to update the original format with new talent and film the program in front of a live audience at Walt Disney World's MGM Studios in Orlando, Florida. Shelly read that there were 10 spots open for kids with talent. She believed the producers would be interested in Christina.

Once again Christina and her mother drove to Pittsburgh for an audition. Shelly cautioned her daughter not to be too excited—there would be a lot of competition. In addition to singing, the cast members were also expected to dance and act. Christina didn't let that

Christina sings the national anthem at the Pittsburgh Pirates home opener in April 2000. She began such appearances when she was just 10 years old, long before having gained national recognition.

daunt her. She decided to audition by singing another Whitney Houston song, "I Wanna Dance with Somebody." She was one of 500 girls who tried out that day.

After her audition, the producers thanked her and told her that they would inform the candidates of their decision by mail. Once again Christina had to wait on pins and needles to find out about her future.

Two weeks later, the letter arrived. The news it delivered wasn't what Christina had hoped to hear. The producers thought that, at 10 years old, she was too young for the show. She hadn't made the final cut for one of the spots on *Mickey Mouse Club*—or even done well enough to have a screen test. The only consolation for Christina was that the producers

After auditioning for a role on Mickey Mouse Club, *Christina hoped she would get to work in the world-renowned theme park. While her first try led to one of her biggest disappointments, two years later she won the part.*

seemed genuinely impressed by her talent. In the letter, they promised to keep her in mind for any future openings on the show.

Fortunately, there was happy news at home that lifted Christina's spirits a little. Her mother had been dating a paramedic named Jim Kearns. The couple had decided to get married. Christina knew Jim well and adored him. Her new stepfather was also supportive of her singing.

Christina and Rachel gained younger siblings over the next few years. Shelly and Jim had another daughter, Stephanie, as well as twin boys, Casey and Robert. This made Christina the oldest of five children.

Christina was 12 when she arrived home

from school one day to see an envelope from Disney in the mail. Curious, she opened it. She had to read the letter three times before she could fully take in the words printed there. Disney wanted her to have a screen test. More than two years after her audition for *Mickey Mouse Club*, she was going to get another chance to become a cast member! To her complete astonishment, the Disney executives had remembered her. Christina began to prepare for the trip to Orlando for the screen test. She bought new clothes, got a haircut, and sang every chance she got.

When Christina and her mother arrived at Disney World, they found a car waiting to take them to their hotel. They were given passes to all the attractions at the theme park and were treated like celebrities. Christina was excited to be there, but she was also distracted by the prospect of her screen test the next day. She'd be terribly disappointed if she didn't make it this time.

The next morning a car picked up Christina and her mother at their hotel and drove them to the studio. Christina met the producers of the show, and then it was time for her audition. She had three minutes to sing.

Afterward an exhausted Christina waited. Her mother hugged her, and together, they tried not to be too nervous. They'd know in just a few minutes what the Disney people thought.

Soon the door opened and both the director and producer of the show entered. The two executives were smiling as they invited the young singer to join the cast. Christina was so excited, she screamed. She couldn't believe it was finally happening—she was going to be a Mouseketeer!

4

MICKEY MOUSE CLUB

*M*ickey Mouse Club (*MMC*) was entering its sixth season and was one of the most successful programs on the Disney Channel. At age 12, Christina was one of the youngest members of the cast. The show was filmed in front of a live audience at Walt Disney World's MGM Studios. This meant Christina was going to be face-to-face with her audience, an experience that she always enjoyed.

The idea behind the show was to provide simple, family-oriented entertainment. The Mouseketeers sang, danced, performed comedy skits, and mixed with celebrity guests. The show also focused on social issues such as drug use and peer pressure, as well as typical situations kids might find themselves in at school and home.

Christina was in her element. She was going to be paid to do what she loved more than anything—perform. After the contracts had been signed, she and her mother had some major decisions to make. Since the show was filmed in Orlando, Christina would have to move to Florida for the summer. The money she earned would be put in the bank for college.

Christina (middle right) poses with other Mouseketeers, including good friend Britney Spears (front right). When the show ended, many cast members found stardom in acting or music.

Christina also decided to keep the news about her new job a secret. She had learned from past experience that many of her peers were bound to be jealous. Even though a part of her longed to tell everyone about her success, she sensed it might be better to keep the news to herself for a while.

As soon as school ended that June, Christina and Shelly headed to Florida. They moved into an apartment near the MGM Studios. "It was so cool, going to work at Disney World," Christina told *Teen Beat* magazine. "It was such fun, being a part of the show, and being in Orlando. And working with such wonderful people—we were just like brothers and sisters!"

Meeting the other cast members was one of the best parts of becoming a Mouseketeer. Among them were Britney Spears, Keri Russell, J. C. Chasez, and several other newcomers: Nikki DeLoach, Ryan Gosling, Tate Lynche, and T. J. Fantini. Like Christina, the other Mouseketeers were very talented kids who could sing, dance, and act. And like Christina, many of them would later become famous. J. C. and newcomer Justin Timberlake later became part of the wildly successful boy band 'N Sync. Keri Russell established herself as a major acting talent when she landed the starring role on the TV show *Felicity*. Christina became especially good friends with Britney Spears, who later also became a record-breaking solo artist.

Christina's first season as a Mouseketeer was a very busy one. The producers planned to tape a whole season of shows over the summer. This meant that Christina and the other members of the show wouldn't have to miss much school, but it also meant that each day was filled with work—rehearsals, learning new songs and skits, then taping the show. Christina was exhausted by the work schedule, but exhilarated by everything she was doing.

Christina considers her time on the set of *Mickey Mouse Club* an invaluable period in her career. She developed dancing and acting skills, and improved her breathing and vocalizing techniques. She also learned a little about performing comedy. (In one skit she actually had a pie thrown in her face.)

"It was a wonderful education for me," she told a reporter at the *Los Angeles Times*. "Being on the show gave me so much confidence in myself. It taught me so much about discipline and hard work—the lessons I would need if I was really going to succeed in the music business."

When that exciting first summer came to an end, Christina reluctantly packed up her things. She hated having to say good-bye to her new friends, and she dreaded returning to school in Wexford. She knew that the word about her job at Disney would spread like wildfire once the new television season began in the fall. Christina didn't know what kind of reaction to expect from her peers back home, but she had a feeling they wouldn't respond very enthusiastically.

When the first episode of *Mickey Mouse Club* aired that October, the reaction was just as Christina had feared. Some friends stuck by her, but others acted distant and aloof. Just like before, many kids ignored her or made fun of her.

When articles about Christina began to appear in local newspapers, things only got worse. And since she was now on television each week, each of her appearances seemed to trigger a whole new wave of resentment.

Luckily, Christina was still in touch with her friends from *MMC*. Several of them had experienced similar problems at home, and their sympathy helped Christina make it through some rough times.

It also helped that Christina was starting to receive fan mail from kids who had seen her on TV. Christina delighted in the attention and the enthusiastic response from these viewers, especially since she was having so much trouble at school. She did her best to reply to each and every letter, even though she had to spend a lot of her free time writing in order to answer all her mail.

One day a different sort of letter arrived at her home. It was from Steve Kurtz, a businessman who wanted to be her agent. He believed that he could help turn Christina into a major star.

Shelly and Christina met with Kurtz several times. Shelly carefully thought through his offer to represent her daughter. She was aware that signing with an agent was a big step. But Christina was still so young. Shelly wanted to be sure that her daughter continued her education.

At the same time there was no denying that Christina was very driven. Nothing was going to stop her from pursuing her dream of becoming a professional singer. Finally, Shelly gave her consent, and the contract with Kurtz was signed. The next step was for Christina to record a demo tape in a studio. Kurtz would then send the tape to record companies and try to interest them in his young client.

Kurtz warned Christina that it would probably be a while before they heard from any of the record labels. He also reminded her that the music industry was a very competitive business, and Christina herself was young and relatively inexperienced. This would make it risky for a record company to take a chance on her.

In the meantime, Christina waited eagerly for school to end that spring. She couldn't wait to return to Orlando to see the other cast members and tape the next season of *Mickey Mouse Club.* "The show was like summer camp, all of us coming together," Christina remembers. "We'd start the school year late, and leave early in the spring."

However, when Christina and her family arrived in Orlando that spring, disappointing news awaited them. The Disney executives announced that the company had decided that this would be the last season of the show.

Christina and the other Mouseketeers were devastated. The one consoling thought for all of them was that the show's cancellation might open doors and create new opportunities for them. Christina later told one interviewer, "We used to joke about backstage and say, 'Whenever the show ends, we'll all go off on our separate ways and become stars.' We're all so dedicated and driven—I'm not surprised at any of the success of my co-Mouseketeers."

The young cast members pushed themselves that summer. They worked very hard during the days, and in their free time they had a blast together, listening to music, exploring Orlando, and just goofing around.

Christina's confidence in her own talent was growing. The Disney vocal coach with whom she was working had noticed a big difference in the teenager's singing skills since the previous year. Her technique had matured a lot, and her ability to hold a note was impressive.

When that summer ended, Christina returned

home, and tried to remain optimistic about her career. Kurtz reported that her demo tape hadn't sparked any interest from American record companies yet, but there were opportunities in Japan. He explained that many American performers had achieved success in Japan, where there is a big demand for Western music. Kurtz had a hunch that Christina's demo would interest record companies in Japan, and he planned to send her tape to them.

Kurtz's instincts soon proved correct. After hearing Christina's demo, a Japanese pop star, Keizo Nakanishi, got in touch with Kurtz, saying that he wanted to record a duet with the young American singer.

Christina was delighted to have a new opportunity. The song that Keizo Nakanishi had selected was "All I Wanna Do." Christina recorded her part in the United States, then sent it to Japan. Soon after, she and her mother flew to Tokyo. There she taped the music video that would accompany the release of the record.

When "All I Wanna Do" was released later that spring, the song became an instant hit in Japan. The record company wanted Christina to fly back to Japan to tour with Keizo and perform the duet.

Christina was excited about the chance to tour with a major pop star. Then her manager relayed more exciting news: he'd booked a spot for her at the Golden Stag Festival, a well-known music festival in Romania. She'd be appearing on the same bill, or program, as several famous American singers, including Sheryl Crow and Diana Ross.

That summer Christina returned to Japan. The tour with Keizo was a great experience. The teenage singer knew that she was singing

well, and each day she grew more polished and confident of her talent.

Still she couldn't help feeling nervous about the festival coming up in Romania. In Japan she was performing a duet with another singer, who was older and very experienced. But in Romania, she'd be singing solo, completely on her own.

Right from the start, Christina found Romania quite different from what she'd encountered in Japan. For one thing, the accommodations were a lot less luxurious, with fewer amenities for travelers. Many of the Romanian citizens she saw appeared very poor.

Despite these less-than-ideal conditions, the

In Japan 14-year-old Christina recorded her first single, a duet with pop star Keizo Nakanishi, with whom she later toured.

A group of young Romanian singers, wearing traditional costumes, are part of an effort to preserve local customs. Christina was surprised to see how poor the Romanian people were in general, but delighted by their enthusiastic response to her performance.

music festival was an enormous event. When Christina arrived to sing, she was amazed by the size of the crowd—more than 10,000 people had come to hear the performers.

With butterflies fluttering inside her stomach, Christina walked onto the stage. As always, her nerves settled as she launched into her first song. By the time she finished, she was completely relaxed and smiling broadly. The audience was applauding enthusiastically, letting her know that they wanted to hear more.

Christina was scheduled to perform two songs. For her next and final number, she impulsively jumped off the stage. She strolled through the massive crowd, singing as she walked along. The audience went wild. Many people jumped up and tried to touch her as she went past. According to some accounts, Christina's impromptu gesture almost started a riot.

When her performance ended, the audience's applause rocked the concert site. They loved this young girl from the United States. Exhilarated, Christina hurried offstage, where she found her mother looking very upset. Shelly told Christina that she had just taken a risk by walking among the huge crowd. Something could have happened to her.

Christina promised her mother that she wouldn't leave the stage again during a performance. Still she didn't let Shelly's warnings dampen her high spirits. Christina had just won herself thousands of new fans—and she was on top of the world.

5

"REFLECTION"

C hristina returned from her trip to Japan and Romania feeling both exhausted and elated. She'd had a wonderful time performing for the foreign audiences and was hoping that her successful trip might produce an offer from a Japanese record company. Better yet, maybe the publicity from the tour would attract interest from an American record company. But once again her manager warned that it was all going to take time.

Christina had some trouble adjusting to school that fall. She'd just had the extraordinary experience of performing in front of thousands of people. Now she was faced with the very ordinary experience of going back to high school in Wexford.

Once again she found herself uncertain about how much to reveal to her peers about her trip and her career. She handled the pressure by trying to stay focused on her schoolwork and working on improving her technical skills as a singer. In her free time, she hung around at home or went to the mall with her friends.

Kurtz was thinking carefully about Christina's career, too.

Christina's popularity with American fans began with the release of "Reflection" from the animated movie Mulan. *"The song's theme—the struggle to establish your identity—was something I could really relate to as a teenage girl myself," she said.*

He arranged for her to record a new demo tape. This one was designed to show off Christina's maturation and development as an artist. He sent the new demo to several record companies, hoping that it, along with Christina's experience as a Mouseketeer on the Disney show, would help to get her noticed.

At about the same time, a very significant change was brewing in the music industry. Alternative rock, which had dominated the scene for some time, was beginning to fade. New pop bands such as the Backstreet Boys and the Spice Girls had become hugely successful. The members of another boy band, 'N Sync, were also on the verge of becoming megastars. As a result, American record companies were suddenly scrambling to find young talent. They were especially hungry for singers who would appeal to the teen and preteen crowd.

Kurtz had noticed this new trend. He sensed

Christina had totally charmed audiences in Japan and Romania, but her future in the United States was still uncertain.

that it was just a matter of time before his client got her big break.

At a recording company, the Artist and Repertoire (A&R) department is responsible for signing up new acts. RCA Record's A&R director, Ron Fair, was among those looking for young, new talent to ride the wave of interest in pop music. When he heard Christina's new demo, he was immediately impressed. "She was fearless," Fair recalled later. "She had perfect intonation and command of her instrument that normally you would see in someone a lot older. I was struck by her amazing voice, her budding beauty, and I decided to take a shot and sign her to a demo deal."

The surprising success of the Spice Girls signaled a significant change of direction in the music industry. The group's popularity created opportunities for new artists like Christina.

Donny and Marie Osmond pose for a photo in 1998 as they promote their new TV talk show, The Donny and Marie Show. *As part of Disney's promotion for* Mulan, *Christina sang "Reflection" on* The Donny and Marie Show *and* CBS This Morning.

Christina was ecstatic. A demo deal wasn't the same as a recording contract, but it was definitely a start. As an artist in development, she would get help from RCA to nurture her talent. In a few years, she hoped, the company might even sign her to a real deal.

More opportunities lay just around the corner. Shortly after Ron Fair signed Christina to a demo deal, he received the call from Disney about its need for a vocalist to sing a ballad for *Mulan.*

The soundtrack to *Mulan* was released to

stores on June 2, 1998. Disney promoted its new movie aggressively, which kept Christina incredibly busy.

It was a very exciting time for the young artist. She performed live on *CBS This Morning* as well as *The Donny and Marie Show*. As the film version of *Mulan* became a major hit at the box office, more requests for the young singer to appear on TV and radio, and at other publicity events, flooded her agent's office. The most exciting news was that "Reflection" had sold so many copies, the single had reached number 15 on the Adult/Contemporary chart of record sales. This was an impressive feat for a song from a children's movie.

"Reflection" was nominated for a Golden Globe Award for Best Original Song in a Motion Picture, which gave Christina's career another boost. But as much as she loved being in the spotlight, another part of her was looking forward to the time when the hoopla over *Mulan* died down. She was eager to get started on the exciting task of recording her first CD.

6

NUMBER ONE

By August of 1998, Christina's schedule was finally clear. The first step in the process of making a CD was a huge one: since RCA's recording studios were located on the West Coast, Christina had to temporarily move to Los Angeles. That meant leaving behind her mother, stepfather, and four siblings in Wexford. Even though she was nervous about moving away from her family, Christina was excited, too. "I always dreamed of recording an album before I finished high school," she told a reporter from the *Los Angeles Times*. "And now I'm actually doing it!"

Christina realized that she was extremely fortunate to have been given a recording contract at just 17 years old. She also knew that her own input about the project was going to be limited. The executive producer of the project was Ron Fair, so he'd be the one making the final decisions. But other producers and writers would be involved, too. RCA wanted the CD to be an appealing blend of snappy dance music and soulful ballads. Mixing producers would help to give the album this varied sound.

Christina waves to the crowd during a San Francisco parade in December 1999. With the successful release of her self-titled debut album came a schedule jam-packed with promotional and publicity appearances.

Christina recorded most of the songs during the summer of 1998. The producers decided to simply title the CD *Christina Aguilera*. Such a title would help to introduce the talented singer to the world. RCA planned to include Christina's hit, "Reflection." The album would include other new songs written by well-known songwriters. Among them was Diane Warren, a gifted writer who had created songs for 'N Sync, Aerosmith, and Céline Dion.

Warren's ballad "I Turn to You" is one of the songs that made the final cut of Christina's first CD. It's a slow, melodic piece that opens with the sound of rain and thunder and describes a woman's love for a man who is her "shelter from the storm." Another song on the CD written by Diane is "Somebody's Somebody," a bouncy dance number. One of Christina's favorite songs is "Obvious," written by Heather Holley. It's a simple and gentle ballad about being afraid to show one's feelings.

The pace picks up with several more danceable numbers, "Love Will Find a Way," "What a Girl Wants," and "Come on Over (All I Want Is You)." They're all catchy, up-tempo songs. Christina has described "What a Girl Wants" as especially fun to sing. It's a song about young women being strong and clear about their own wishes and desires.

The young singer was very pleased with the compilation of songs. However, the producers wanted to include one song that initially made her uneasy. It would later become her biggest hit from the recording. "Genie in a Bottle" is a mid-tempo song about a female genie who refuses to come out of the bottle to be a man's slave. Instead she wants the man to be the one to please her.

When Christina first heard the song's lyrics, she worried that some of her listeners would misconstrue the meaning of the song. Its message seemed overtly sexual. "At first I was a little afraid that some people might not completely get where I'm coming from in the song," she explained in an interview with *Billboard* magazine. "It's about self-respect. It's about not giving in to temptation until you're respected."

Christina was also concerned that the song was too "pop." It's easy to sing, demanding little from someone with her vocal range. The talented artist wanted her first album to show off her abilities, not encourage people to dismiss her as just another pop singer.

Eventually, Ron Fair persuaded her that "Genie in a Bottle" was exactly what the debut album needed. "Christina was just 18, and she needed to connect with her audience and there was never any question that ["Genie in the Bottle"] was the way to do it," Fair said. "In our business it's more important to start off with a number one record on a debut act than it is to start off with a great song. But it's still great sugar candy."

Recording the album took six months of long, hard work. Because various producers were involved in the project, Christina spent a lot of time traveling back and forth between several recording studios around LA. When she wasn't working, she spent her time being tutored so that she could finish high school.

Christina also enjoyed being exposed to all kinds of new music while living in LA. She especially liked a band called Limp Bizkit, whose music mixes rock and hip-hop.

As a new recording artist, Christina was

Eager fans line up to get Christina's autograph. "I know some people hate [being a celebrity]," she told an interviewer. "But not me. I've been waiting for this moment all my life."

learning a great deal about being a professional singer. "I wanted to start belting with the very first verse, and [Ron Fair taught] me how to not let the cat out of the bag too soon, how to keep it soft at first," she said.

The people at RCA were very impressed by the young singer. Songwriter Diane Warren described Christina as "just the greatest. When she hits the high notes, you can really feel her talent." In an interview with the *Los Angeles Times*, Steve Kipner, who cowrote "Genie in a Bottle," agreed. "She had abilities you usually only see in older, more experienced artists," Kipner remarked. "She used lessons she'd learned from artists like Mariah Carey and Chaka Khan, and created her own, amazing sound. She's just extraordinary."

The next phase of the project was shooting the album cover. Christina had a complete makeover, which included making her hair more blonde and highlighting her deep blue eyes with makeup. RCA also helped her create a distinct "look" for herself—mostly crop tops and pants and skirts that hug her hips and show off her naturally slim figure.

When the record and cover shoot were completed that December, Christina felt satisfied. Everyone had worked hard, and the producers at RCA were hopeful that the album would be a success. But still she couldn't help feeling nervous about what would happen when her debut album hit the stores. "I just hope everyone likes the record," she confessed to *Teen Beat* magazine. "It means a lot to me to please the fans."

Christina had to make one more trip to California, this time to film the video that would be released along with the first single,

"Genie in a Bottle." Directed by Diane Martel, who had worked with big stars like Mariah Carey, the video follows the song's story line about a genie who is found by a master. The genie tells the boy that she's not going to come out of the bottle until he promises to treat her with respect and grant her wishes. Christina prepared for the video shoot by rehearsing dance routines and working with a choreographer. She personally selected the teen who would play her love interest in the video, a performer named Ryan McTavish.

The video was shot at night on the beach in Malibu, a town in southern California. Christina wore a genie outfit with a halter top made of beads. It was cold that night, and Christina spent much of the time huddled under blankets. The filming went on through the night, with dozens of takes and retakes from various camera angles. It was tiring work, but Christina recognized that it was a very important part of the release of her single. With the significance of MTV, the music video could make or break her career.

The single "Genie in a Bottle" was released to radio stations on June 22, 1999. Just as Ron Fair had predicted, the bouncy pop song quickly became the big hit of the summer. It shot to the top of the *Billboard* chart, the list that tracks the sales of new releases for the music industry. The single eventually sold more than a million copies. The music video was just as successful. In its first week of release, it reached the top 10 on MTV's popular show *Total Request Live*.

Mademoiselle magazine was instantly impressed. "Move over, Mariah Carey!" the magazine trumpeted. Even before Christina's

album was released, reviewers were describing the young singer's voice as "rich" with "range, maturity, and sensuality." *Mademoiselle* named her one of the people to watch in the new millennium, while *Time* magazine called her a "young Mariah Carey."

By the time the album *Christina Aguilera* was released in August, it seemed that everyone in the country already knew who the young singer was. "Genie in a Bottle" had been playing on radios everywhere for months; Christina had been interviewed by MTV and dozens of radio stations; and she'd taped appearances on *The Tonight Show with Jay Leno*, UPN's *Summer Music Mania '99*, and the *1999 Teen Choice Awards*. That

Christina gives an energized performance at the 1999 Teen Choice Awards, one of many appearances made to publicize her first album.

summer she had also appeared at Lilith Fair, a concert series organized by the singer Sarah McLachlan, which featured only female singers. For her Lilith Fair appearances, Christina was accompanied simply by a pianist. The idea of not having a band to back her up might have daunted many young singers, but Christina saw it instead as an opportunity to be daring and prove that she was more than just another teenage pop singer.

"I'm not going to be singing 'Genie in a Bottle,'" she told an interviewer on MTV beforehand. "It's a time where . . . I can . . . really sing my heart out to just piano and vocal. It's just a piano and a mike, and that's it. I'll get bluesy with Etta James's 'At Last,' which is one of my favorite songs."

Christina Aguilera stayed at *Billboard*'s number one spot for a week. After that it stayed in the top 10 on the charts for several weeks. Five weeks after its release, the album had sold more than 2 million copies. By February 2000, it had sold more than 7 million copies.

Despite the album's amazing success, the reviews weren't all positive. *Entertainment Weekly* described the collection as "frustratingly erratic," and a reviewer at *People* called the rhythm-and-blues arrangements "watery."

But none of the negative comments did the least bit of damage to Christina's skyrocketing career. She was having a great time and completely enjoying her newfound fame.

Unlike some pop stars who hid behind sunglasses or bodyguards, Christina was thrilled when some young fans who had seen her video recognized her for the first time. "They had just bought my single and had it with them," Christina explains. "Then they went out and bought a disposable camera to take my picture." "I know some people hate that," she told another interviewer. "But not me. I've been waiting for this moment all my life."

"What a Girl Wants"

As 1999 came to a close, Christina celebrated her 19th birthday. That year she made a guest appearance on the hit TV show *Beverly Hills 90210*, attended the European MTV Awards in Ireland, appeared in the Macy's Thanksgiving Day Parade in New York City, and released a Christmas song. She also shared the stage with President Bill Clinton and First Lady Hillary Rodham Clinton during the finale of the "Christmas in Washington" show. It had been a grueling schedule. As the new year arrived, her whirlwind pace showed no sign of slowing. MTV invited her to help the network ring in the new millennium in New York City's Times Square. She also began planning to tour in the new year, opening for the group TLC. However, the biggest news of all hadn't yet reached Christina.

Each year in January, the National Academy of Recording Arts and Sciences announces its nominations for the Grammy Awards. These honors are given in a variety of categories to artists considered worthy of recognition. On January 4, 2000, Christina was named one of the nominees in the category of Best New Artist.

The enthusiasm Christina exudes during the Super Bowl halftime performance with Enrique Iglesias in January 2000 has always marked her appearances.

For Christina, this was truly a dream come true. She remembered watching on TV when her idol Mariah Carey received the same award. Christina hoped to win, but she knew the competition was very stiff. The other four nominees were Christina's friend and former co-Mouseketeer Britney Spears; Macy Gray; Kid Rock; and Susan Tedeschi.

The 42nd Annual Grammy Award show was broadcast on February 23. Christina wore a short, beaded dress designed by Versace. Lilith Fair participants Sheryl Crow, Melissa Etheridge, and Sarah McLachlan had been chosen to present the award for Best New Artist. As they stepped up to the microphone to read the winner's name, Christina wasn't too nervous. Experts predicted that Britney Spears or Macy Gray would walk away as the winner.

Suddenly, Christina's name rang out in the crowded auditorium. She was stunned. As she hurried up to the stage to accept the award, she had the presence of mind to mouth an ecstatic "Hi Mom!" to the TV cameras.

Twenty-four hours later she was still in shock over winning the Grammy. "I didn't expect it all," she told an interviewer. "[But] I worked really, really hard on my career this year and it was good to be recognized for it." This was not the only time Christina's hard work was recognized. In April 2000, she won the New Entertainer of the Year Award at the American Latino Media Arts Awards.

With prestigious awards and a successful recording career, it appears that Christina has accomplished more in her teens than most people do in a lifetime. After the Grammy Awards, the winning singer embarked on a promotional tour in the United States throughout the summer and fall months.

In September 2000, Christina released her first Spanish-language album, *Mi Reflejo* (My Reflection). The Latin-flavored album holds special meaning for her. In recent years, the music industry has experienced a surge of popularity in Latin music, performed by artists such as Jennifer Lopez, Ricky Martin, Carlos Santana, and Enrique Iglesias. Christina has a very personal reason to pursue a Spanish album. Her father is Ecuadorian, which makes her half-Latino. Even though she has had little contact with Fausto Aguilera since her parents' divorce, she still wants to explore her roots. She began studying Spanish and Latin culture in preparation both for a Spanish version of "Genie in a Bottle," which was released early in 2000, and for *Mi Reflejo*.

In the meantime, Christina has a few more normal, teenage goals. She managed to earn her high school diploma by being tutored, but so far she has not had time to learn to drive. In addition to getting a driver's license (and a cute sports car to go with it), she might some-day go to college.

Christina has moved into an apartment in New York City, which is just a ferry ride away from where she was born on Staten Island. She's not in New York very often, but she's glad it's relatively close to her family in Wexford, Pennsylvania. Christina remains close to her family, especially her mom. "My mother has given me a lot of strength," she says. "When things get overwhelming, I know that I have her support."

In some ways, Christina's own life resembles a fairy tale, as if a genie has magically

Christina poses with the New Entertainer of the Year Award she received at the American Latino Media Arts Awards in April 2000. Although she's had little contact with her birth father, Christina is eager to explore her Latin roots.

granted all her wishes. But as she points out, her success is the result of hard work and sheer determination, with a little luck thrown in for good measure. The determined singer has always pushed herself, from the time she was a little girl who dreamed about making it to the set of *Star Search.* And she has always managed to stay focused on her goals, despite the formidable obstacles of her parents' divorce and the jealousy of her peers.

At this point, Christina's career path could take any direction. She has said that she might someday accept one of the many movie roles she's been offered or take a part in a Broadway musical. But for now she wants to concentrate on making music, particularly on writing her own songs. As she herself admitted, "Music will always be number one, what I always want to be known for."

CHRONOLOGY

1980	Born Christina Maria Aguilera on December 18 on Staten Island, New York.
1987	Parents divorce.
1989	Appears on the TV show *Star Search*.
1990	Sings national anthem at Pittsburgh Steelers, Penguins, and Pirates' games.
1993	Joins cast of Disney's *Mickey Mouse Club*.
1994	Signs Steve Kurtz as manager; *Mickey Mouse Club* is canceled in October.
1995	Records duet "All I Wanna Do" with Japanese star Keizo Nakanishi; tours Japan with Keizo; sings at Golden Stag Festival in Romania.
1998	Records "Reflection" for the soundtrack of *Mulan*, which soars up the charts and is nominated for a Golden Globe Award for Best Original Song in a Motion Picture; signs a contract with RCA Records.
1999	Single "Genie in a Bottle" is released and sells a million copies in a week; debut album, *Christina Aguilera*, is released and eventually sells more than seven million copies.
2000	Wins the Grammy Award for Best New Artist and American Latino Media Arts Award for New Entertainer of the Year; releases Spanish-language album *Mi Reflejo* and Christmas album, *My Kind of Christmas*.

ACCOMPLISHMENTS

Singles

1995   "All I Wanna Do" with Keizo Nakanishi (Japan only)

1999   "Genie in a Bottle"
           "What a Girl Wants"
           "The Christmas Song"
           "Genio Atrapado" (Spanish version of "Genie in a Bottle")

2000   "I Turn to You"
           "Come On Over (All I Want Is You)"

Albums

1999   *Christina Aguilera*

2000   *Mi Reflejo*
           My Kind of Christmas

Soundtracks

1998   "Reflection" from *Mulan*

1999   "We're a Miracle" from *Pokemon: The First Movie*

2000   "Don't Make Me Love You," from *The Next Best Thing*

Awards

2000   Grammy Award for Best New Artist

           Blockbuster Entertainment Award for Favorite New Female Artist

           Blockbuster Entertainment Award for Favorite Single for "Genie in a Bottle"

           ALMA Award for New Entertainer of the Year

FURTHER READING

Gabriel, Jan. *Backstage Pass: Christina Aguilera.* New York: Scholastic Books, 2000.

Golden, Anna Louise. *Christina Aguilera: An Unauthorized Biography.* New York: St. Martin's Press, 2000.

Harrington, Richard. "Christina Aguilera's Fast Track: Ex-Mouseketeer Has the Voice to Pull Away from the Teen Pop Pack." *Washington Post,* February 13, 2000.

MacDermot, Molly. *Christina Aguilera: The Unofficial Book.* New York: Billboard Books, 2000.

Murphy, Catherine. *Christina Aguilera.* New York: Andrews McMeel, 2000.

Robb, Jackie. *Christina Aguilera: An Unauthorized Biography.* New York: HarperCollins, 1999.

INDEX

ABOUT THE AUTHOR

A former children's book editor, SUSAN KORMAN is the author of more than 20 books for children. She lives in Bucks County, Pennsylvania, with her husband, three children, and two cats.